Computer Forensics with FTK

Enhance your computer forensics knowledge through illustrations, tips, tricks, and practical real-world scenarios

Fernando Carbone

BIRMINGHAM - MUMBAI

Computer Forensics with FTK

First published: March 2014

Production Reference: 1130314

Published by Packt Publishing Ltd.
Livery Place
35 Livery Street
Birmingham B3 2PB, UK.

ISBN 978-1-78355-902-2

www.packtpub.com

Cover Image by Eleanor Leonne Bennett (eleanor.ellieonline@gmail.com)

Credits

Author

Fernando Carbone

Reviewers

Gretchen Gueguen

Jacob Heilik

Faraz Siddiqui

Acquisition Editors

Anthony Albuquerque

Richard Harvey

Content Development Editor

Sruthi Kutty

Technical Editors

Pragnesh Bilimoria

Nikhil Potdukhe

Copy Editors

Dipti Kapadia

Kirti Pai

Project Coordinator

Sageer Parkar

Proofreader

Simran Bhogal

Indexers

Mariammal Chettiyar

Rekha Nair

Graphics

Abhinash Sahu

Production Coordinator

Aditi Gajjar Patel

Cover Work

Aditi Gajjar Patel

About the Author

Fernando Carbone is the Director of the Forensic Technology Services practice in PwC Brazil, based in São Paulo, with more than 15 years of work experience divided between information security and computer forensics. He specializes in assisting companies in digital crime investigations, electronic discovery process, and litigation technical support.

He has worked in the financial industry (Unibanco and Itau) for seven years, and has participated in investigation projects and computer forensics involving more than 100,000 assets. He was responsible for the creation of the incident response team at these institutions.

He is currently a professor of the computer forensics post-graduation course at Universidade Presbiteriana Mackenzie and Impact Tecnologia. He is certified in EnCE, ACE, CHFI, CEH, Security+, CoBIT, ITIL, ISO 27002, and others. He has a Network Computers degree from Instituto Brasileiro de Tecnologia Avançada (IBTA), a post-graduate degree in Information Security, and a post-graduate degree in Project Management, both from IBTA.

This is his first book.

I would like to thank my family for all the support and encouragement throughout the production of the book, and my friends of PwC who helped me in this journey.

Thanks to Juliana D'addio for supporting me in the project and contributing to the review.

I want to mention and acknowledge the names of those who helped me write this book, to express gratitude for their effort. They are José Francci, Júlio Benatto, Alan Lai, and João Castilho for the technical discussions on the subject that helped in the preparation of the chapters, and Edgar D'andrea, a partner at PwC, for believing in the idea of the book and giving me the opportunity for my research.

About the Reviewers

Gretchen Gueguen is an archives and library consultant, specializing in digital libraries and technology. She has held the position of Digital Archivist at the University of Virginia where she created the first born-digital archives management and digital forensics programs. She has previously worked on digital library projects at East Carolina University and the University of Maryland. She began her journey in digital humanities at the Maryland Institute for Technology in Humanities, working on the Thomas MacGreevy Archive.

Jacob Heilik has worked for 35 years in law enforcement (regulatory compliance and criminal investigation) with the Canadian Federal Government. The last 10 years of his career were spent learning and practicing digital forensics—searching and seizing in the field, analyzing in the lab, and managing a talented team of examiners and analysts. Since retiring from public service in 2009, he has concentrated his efforts on improving digital forensic skills in law enforcement.

Striving to be a positive influence, aiming to improve everything he is involved with, he has helped to train officers from around the world, being involved with projects sponsored by Interpol, Europol, the European Cybercrime Training and Education Group, and University College Dublin.

Faraz Siddiqui has obtained a BS in Forensic Chemistry. Somewhere along his career, he decided to go back to school to pursue something more technical. He obtained an MS in Digital Forensics and has been working in the Computer Security field ever since. When he is not occupied with his obsessions about the latest technology, he loves to spend his time with his beautiful wife and children.

www.packtpub.com

Support files, eBooks, discount offers and more

You might want to visit www.packtpub.com for support files and downloads related to your book.

Did you know that Packt offers eBook versions of every book published, with PDF and ePub files available? You can upgrade to the eBook version at www.packtpub.com and as a print book customer, you are entitled to a discount on the eBook copy. Get in touch with us at service@packtpub.com for more details.

At www.packtpub.com, you can also read a collection of free technical articles, sign up for a range of free newsletters and receive exclusive discounts and offers on Packt books and eBooks.

www.packtpub.com

Do you need instant solutions to your IT questions? PacktLib is Packt's online digital book library. Here, you can access, read and search across Packt's entire library of books.

Why Subscribe?

- Fully searchable across every book published by Packt
- Copy and paste, print and bookmark content
- On demand and accessible via web browser

Free Access for Packt account holders

If you have an account with Packt at www.packtpub.com, you can use this to access PacktLib today and view nine entirely free books. Simply use your login credentials for immediate access.

Table of Contents

Preface

Welcome to *Computer Forensics with FTK*. This book has specially been created to provide you with all the information you need to get started with the FTK investigation platform. You will learn the basics of computer forensics and how to use the FTK to conduct digital investigations generating court-accepted evidence.

What this book covers

Chapter 1, *Getting Started with Computer Forensics Using FTK*, will get you started with the basic installation and configuration of the FTK and how to prepare your environment lab for digital investigations.

Chapter 2, *Working with FTK Imager*, will teach you how to use the FTK Imager tool to create forensic images of digital devices from volatile data, such as memory.

Chapter 3, *Working with Registry View*, will give a step-by-step demonstration on how to work with Registry View to access and extract relevant information from Windows Registry, and how this information can be important during the investigation process.

Chapter 4, *Working with FTK Forensics*, will cover the main computer forensics process, explaining each step in depth. Also, you will learn some important features of the FTK, such as managing users and processing options.

Chapter 5, *Processing the Case*, will cover how to use the most important features for processing and filtering data during your investigation process. You will learn how to set up the tool to perform data analysis, search information, and bookmark your findings.

Chapter 6, *New Features of FTK 5*, will give an overview of the main new features that have been developed in the FTK 5, and make you understand how these new features can help you during your investigations.

Chapter 7, Working with PRTK, will teach you how to perform a password recovery from files and systems using the PRTK and DNA products, and how it will help you to solve problems when you find some protected information.

What you need for this book

A computer with Windows XP or newer, AccessData Forensic Toolkit 5, some evidence file samples, and an Internet connection.

Who this book is for

Computer forensics with the FTK is great for anyone who wants to conduct digital investigations with an integrated platform. Whether you are new to computer forensics or have some experience, this book will help you get started with the FTK, so you can start analyzing evidence effectively and efficiently.

The book also helps law enforcement officials, corporate security, and IT professionals who need to evaluate the evidentiary value of digital evidences.

Conventions

In this book, you will find a number of styles of text that distinguish between different kinds of information. Here are some examples of these styles, and an explanation of their meaning.

Code words in text, database table names, folder names, filenames, file extensions, pathnames, dummy URLs, user input, and Twitter handles are shown as follows: "These files are located at `C:\Windows\System32\Config`."

Any command-line input or output is written as follows:

```
# [Drive]:\FTK\AccessData Distributed Processing Engine.EXE
```

New terms and **important words** are shown in bold. Words that you see on the screen, in menus or dialog boxes for example, appear in the text like this: "Install the **Distributed Engine** component, as it is necessary for the correct operation of FTK."

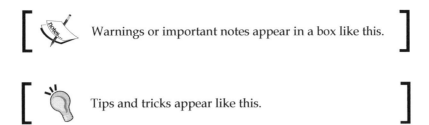

Reader feedback

Feedback from our readers is always welcome. Let us know what you think about this book—what you liked or may have disliked. Reader feedback is important for us to develop titles that you really get the most out of.

To send us general feedback, simply send an e-mail to feedback@packtpub.com, and mention the book title via the subject of your message.

If there is a topic that you have expertise in and you are interested in either writing or contributing to a book, see our author guide on www.packtpub.com/authors.

Customer support

Now that you are the proud owner of a Packt book, we have a number of things to help you to get the most from your purchase.

Downloading color versions of the images for this book

For your convenience we have also provided a PDF that contains higher resolution color versions of the images used in this book. These can be extremely useful as you work through various stages of the project when working with materials or examining small detail changes as we tweak individual parameters. You can download the PDF from https://www.packtpub.com/sites/default/files/downloads/9022OT_ColoredImages.pdf.

Errata

Although we have taken every care to ensure the accuracy of our content, mistakes do happen. If you find a mistake in one of our books—maybe a mistake in the text or the code—we would be grateful if you would report this to us. By doing so, you can save other readers from frustration and help us improve subsequent versions of this book. If you find any errata, please report them by visiting http://www.packtpub.com/submit-errata, selecting your book, clicking on the **errata submission form** link, and entering the details of your errata. Once your errata are verified, your submission will be accepted and the errata will be uploaded on our website, or added to any list of existing errata, under the Errata section of that title. Any existing errata can be viewed by selecting your title from http://www.packtpub.com/support.

Piracy

Piracy of copyright material on the Internet is an ongoing problem across all media. At Packt, we take the protection of our copyright and licenses very seriously. If you come across any illegal copies of our works, in any form, on the Internet, please provide us with the location address or website name immediately so that we can pursue a remedy.

Please contact us at copyright@packtpub.com with a link to the suspected pirated material.

We appreciate your help in protecting our authors, and our ability to bring you valuable content.

Questions

You can contact us at questions@packtpub.com if you are having a problem with any aspect of the book, and we will do our best to address it.

1
Getting Started with Computer Forensics Using FTK

Forensic Toolkit (FTK) is a complete platform for digital investigations, developed to assist the work of professionals working in the information security, technology, and law enforcement sectors.

Through innovative technologies used in filters and the indexing engine, the relevant evidence of investigation cases can be quickly accessed, dramatically reducing the time to perform the analysis.

This chapter will cover the first steps needed to install and configure the FTK tool.

Forensic digital investigations include the following processes:

- Preparation
- Acquisition and preservation
- Analysis
- Reports and presentation

This process will be discussed in more detail in *Chapter 4, Working with FTK Forensics*, with the use of FTK forensics and enterprise editions.

The computer forensics tools need to be kept updated to address issues such as an increasing size of hard drives and the use of encryption in order to reduce the time to perform the data acquisition and analysis.

AccessData has two versions of the platform:

- **FTK forensics**: This version of FTK, which will be covered in this book, has the ability to perform the acquisition and analysis of digital devices such as computer hard drives, USB drives, flash memory devices, smartphones, tablets, and other digital media. Its approach is related to a process called post-mortem computer forensics, which happens when the computer has been powered down.

- **AD Enterprise**: In general, AD Enterprise has the same features as the FTK forensics version plus the ability to analyze multiple computers across your company simultaneously. Another important feature of this version is the ability to acquire and analyze volatile data, such as RAM. The investigation process is totally confidential, and the investigated user will not be aware of the analysis, even if it is done through the network and with the target equipment in use.

 In this book, we will use the solution only in the standalone version.

Downloading FTK

Once the FTK platform has been acquired, AccessData usually sends the DVDs for product installation and the hardware dongle codemeter with the license of the product.

If not, then it is possible to download the FTK directly from the AccessData website. All other products are also available for download.

In this book, we will use FTK Version 5 onwards, and you can download the product from `http://www.accessdata.com/support/product-downloads`.

Prerequisites for FTK

There are two different settings (configuration options) for FTK installation:

- One machine: FTK + database
- Two machines: FTK + database on separate machines

In general, the specification used for FTK with the PostgreSQL database is shown in the following screenshot:

Software	
Operation System	Server 2008 R2 / Windows7 (64-bit)
Hardware	
Processor	Intel® i7, Dual Quad Core Xeon, or AMD equivalent
Memory	32 GB (or more)
OS / Application drive	7200 RPM drive with 64MB cache or SSD drive
Storage for PostgreSQL database	160GB Solid State Drive (SSD) dedicated exclusively to PostgreSQL.
Network Card	Gigabit
HW RAID Controller	Highly recommended if hosting PostgreSQL database. Configure with RAID 5, 6, or 10 avoid RAID0
Temporary Folder Location	SSD drive or RAID0 partition w/ write-through
Drive Configuration	Drive 1: OS Drive 2: PostgreSQL Database (SSD or HW RAID) Drive 3: Case Folder and HD Image Drive 4: Temp Directory (SSD or RAID0)

Note that this is the recommended specification by the vendor. However, the more the processing, memory, and I/O resources available, the faster the analysis.

Installing FTK and the database

FTK installation is quite simple, although the components' installation sequence must be respected. AccessData has created a menu to provide support for the correct installation, as can be seen in the following screenshot:

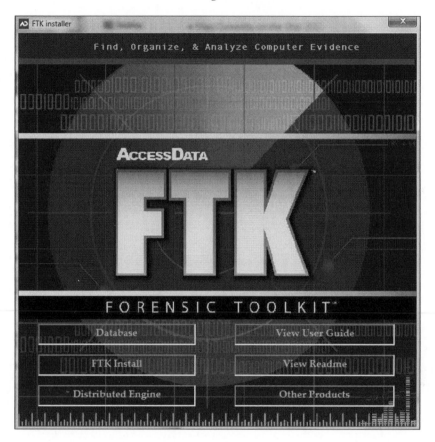

Perform the following steps for installing FTK:

1. Start the installation process by using the **Database** component. You can then enter a password to create the PostgreSQL database admin user.

2. Once the database installation is done, install FTK.

3. Install the **Distributed Engine** component, as it is necessary for the correct operation of FTK.

4. The **View User Guide** installation is optional, but highly recommended.

5. To finish the FTK platform installation process, click on the **Other Products** button and select the components listed as follows:

  ○ **License Manager**: This is the product's license control component

  ○ **Registry Viewer**: This is the Windows registry analysis component

  ○ **PRTK**: This is the password recovery component

  ○ **CodeMeter**: This is the USB CodeMeter hardware driver and management component

  ○ **Imager**: This is the FTK Imager product

 Make sure that you select the correct platform, which can be either 32- or 64-bits, and in case the **Unable to connect to the database requested** error message appears, just change the **RDBMS** option to **PostgresSQL**.

Running FTK for the first time

If the installation has been done correctly, the first step would be to create a user:

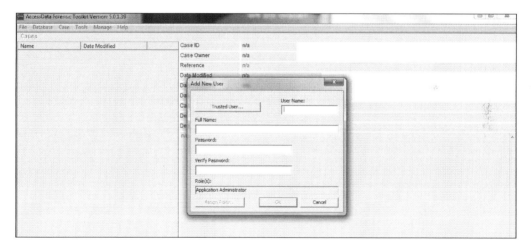

Next, you can complete the fields in the form and then click on **OK** to create the first user. This user will be the application administrator, who will manage the FTK tool. The use of the FTK tool will be discussed in the next few chapters.

Summary

This chapter covered the first necessary steps to be performed in order to use the FTK forensics tool. The first step was to understand the difference between standalone and enterprise platforms as it is extremely important to determine the approach to be used in an investigation. This will certainly impact the time of acquisition and data analysis. Another important point was to consider the hardware prerequisites. Keep in mind that more the computing power the hardware has, the faster is the response of their analysis.

The analysis process is really time-consuming, and if not properly scaled, the hardware can have a negative impact on your project.

In the next chapter, you will use FTK Imager, the free version of the platform, which is commonly used for evidence acquisition and preanalysis of data.

2

Working with FTK Imager

FTK Imager is a free tool that can be downloaded from AccessData on its website, mainly used for conducting acquisition of digital media. To ensure the integrity of the data collected, it creates exact copies (forensic images), known as bit-to-bit or bit stream.

FTK Imager is a powerful, free tool. It allows a preanalysis of the data, information search, and the collection of volatile data such as RAM, along with other features that will be covered through this chapter. You can download FTK Imager as well as other products at `http://www.accessdata.com/support/product-downloads`.

This chapter discusses working with evidence using FTK Imager, allowing you to accomplish the creation of forensic images that meet your exact needs.

You will also be shown how to operate FTK Imager as well as an overview of all the features to understand the process of acquiring digital devices, which is considered one of the most critical factors.

Data storage media

It is important to realize that data acquisition may be performed not only on hard disks, but also across other devices that have the storage capacity, few of which are listed as follows:

- Magnetic media:
    - Floppy disks
    - Hard drives
    - USB/PC cards
    - ZIP and tape drives

- Optical media:
  - CDs
  - CD-Rs and CD-RWs
  - DVDs

- Alternative media:
  - MP3 players
  - Tablets
  - Smartphones
  - Video games, TVs, and so on

FTK Imager has the ability to collect and analyze each of these devices.

During an investigative process, we must look at these items because they may have relevant evidence, not often found in hard disks.

Acquisition tools

FTK Imager makes a bit-for-bit duplicate image of the media, avoiding accidental manipulation of the original evidence. The forensic image is an identical copy of the original device, which includes the file slack and unallocated space, and allows for the recovery of deleted files. The forensic duplication allows you to conduct the investigation process using the image, preserving the original media.

The analysis of the acquired image can be performed later in the FTK, which allows for a much more detailed investigation and the generation of the final report of the information found.

When you use FTK Imager to create a forensic image of a hard drive or other electronic device, ensure that you are using a hardware-based write blocker. By doing this, you can be certain that the system does not alter the original source at the time of attaching it to your computer.

In the following picture, you can see a sample of the write blocker device:

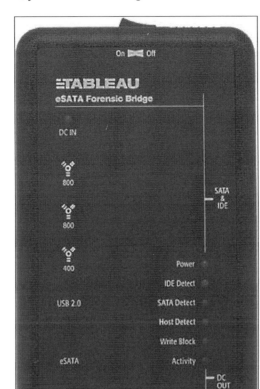

Image formats

FTK Imager can support almost all types of images used in the market. The main types are filesystems supported, Imager creates formats supported, and Imager read formats. These are listed as follows:

- Filesystems supported FTK Imager supports the following filesystems:
  - DVD (UDF)
  - CD (ISO, Joliet, and CDFS)
  - FAT (12, 16, and 32)

- ○ exFAT
- ○ VXFS
- ○ EXT (2, 3, and 4)
- ○ NTFS (and NTFS compressed)
- ○ HFS, HFS+, and HFSX

- FTK Imager can create evidence files of the following formats:
  - ○ E01, S01, and L01
  - ○ AFF
  - ○ AD1
  - ○ RAW/DD

- FTK Imager read formats — in the following screenshot you can see all the formats that FTK Imager supports to read:

```
All Files (*.*)
E01 Images (*.e01)
SMART Images (*.s01)
Advanced Forensic Format Images (*.aff)
Virtual Hard Disk (*.vhd)
ICS Images (*.I01)
SafeBack / SnapBack Images (*.001)
Tar Archive (*.tar)
Zip Archive (*.zip)
AccessData Logical Image (*.AD1)
VMDK Virtual Drive (*.vmdk)
Ghost Raw Image (*.gho)
Raw CD/DVD image (*.iso; *.img; *.bin; *.tao; *.dao)
Alcohol CD image (*.mds)
DiscJuggler image (*.cdi)
CloneCD image (*.ccd)
Gear CD Image (*.p01)
IsoBuster CD image (*.cue)
Nero CD image (*.nrg)
Philips/OptImage CD image (*.cd)
Pinnacle CD image (*.pdi)
Plextools CD image (*.pxi)
Prassi CD Right Image Plus (*.gcd)
Prassi PrimoDVD Image (*.gi)
Roxio CD Creator Image (*.cif)
Virtual CD image (*.vc4)
WinOnCD image (*.c2d)
Apple Disk Images (*.dmg)
```

The FTK Imager interface

The installation of FTK Imager is very simple and you have the option of using the traditional version, with the need to install the product on your hard disk. Alternatively, you can use the Lite version, which does not need an installation. It has the advantage of allowing FTK Imager to run directly from a USB key, which helps a lot in the field collection process.

The FTK Imager user interface is divided into several panes. The **Evidence Tree** section, the **File List** section, the **Properties** section, and the **Hex Value Interpreter** pane, The **Custom Content Sources** panes, the menu, and the toolbar can all be undocked and resized to best suit your needs. Each can be redocked individually or you can reset the entire view for the next investigation as shown in the following screenshot:

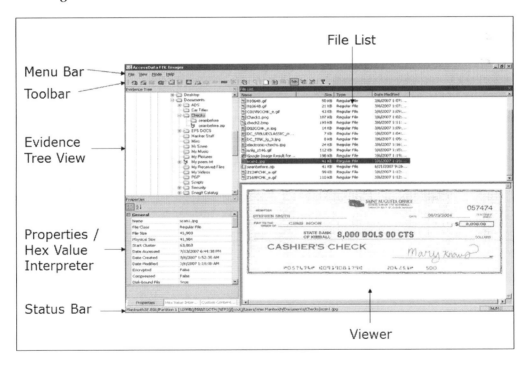

The menu bar

The menu bar can be used to access all the features of FTK Imager. It is always visible and accessible. There are four items on the menu bar:

- **File**: The **File** menu provides access to all the features you can use from the toolbar.

- **View**: The **View** menu allows you to customize the appearance of FTK Imager, which includes showing or hiding panes and control bars.

- **Mode**: The **Mode** menu lets you select the preview mode of the viewer.

- **Help**: The **Help** menu provides access to the FTK Imager user guide, which gives information about the program version and more ways that can assist you.

The toolbar

The toolbar contains all the tools and features that can be accessed from the **File** menu.

The following screenshot provides some basic information on each feature:

The view panes

There are several basic view panes in FTK Imager, which are listed as follows:

- **Evidence Tree**: This pane displays the added evidence items in a hierarchical tree.

- **File List**: This pane shows the files and folders contained in whichever item is currently selected in the **Evidence Tree** pane.

- **Viewer**: This pane shows the content of the currently selected file, based on the selected **Preview Mode** option: **Natural**, **Text**, or **Hex**.

- **Properties/Hex Value Interpreter/Custom Content Sources**: These panes display a variety of information about the object currently selected in either the **Evidence Tree** pane or the **File List** pane, convert hexadecimal values selected in the viewer into decimal integers and possible time and date values, and view the content that will be included in a **Custom Content** image, respectively.

The FTK Imager functionality

You can use FTK Imager to preview a piece of evidence prior to creating the image file(s). You can then choose to image the entire evidence object or choose specific items by selecting **Add to Custom Content (AD1) image**.

Adding and previewing an evidence item

You can either add a single evidence item or several items at one time. The following screenshot shows the procedure in a step-by-step format:

1. Click on the **Add Evidence Item** button on the toolbar.

2. Select the source type you want to preview and then click on **Next**.

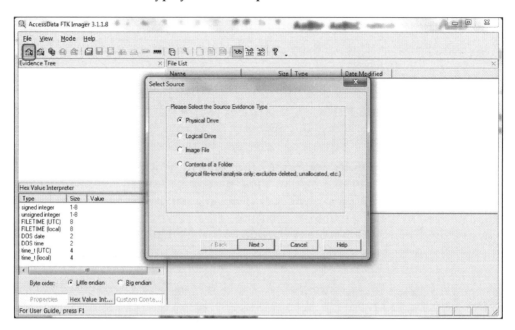

3. Select the drive or browse to the source you want to preview and then click on **Finish**:

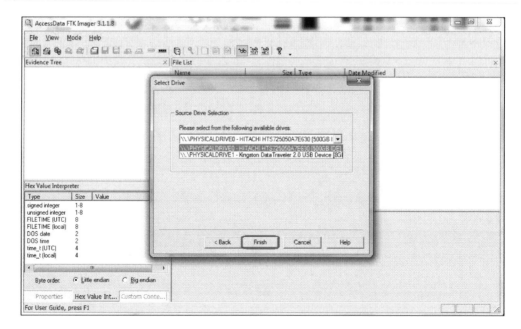

4. The evidence item appears in the **Evidence Tree** pane:

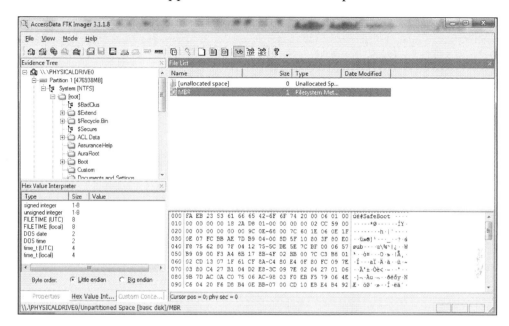

Creating forensic images

Once the item is added to the evidence, you can perform the process of creating a forensic image. FTK Imager allows you to make several different types of forensic images. In addition, drive content and hash lists can be exported.

To create the image, perform the following steps:

1. Click on the **Export Disk Image** button on the toolbar.
2. Click on the **Add...** button.

3. Select the image type and click on **Next**:

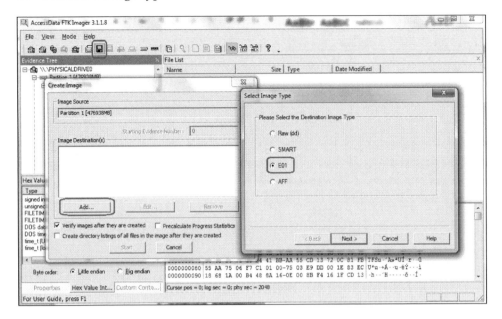

4. Fill the evidence item information and click on **Next**:

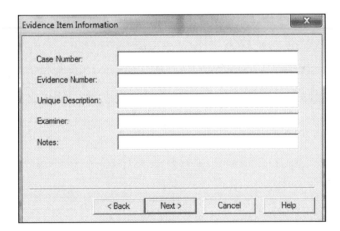

5. Select the destination folder, filename, fragment size, and compression options, and then click on **Finish**:

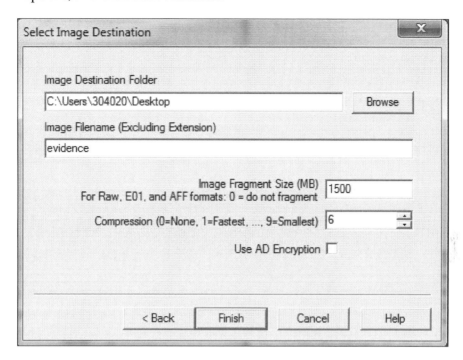

Mounting the image

With the feature of mounting, the forensic images will be allowed to be mounted as a drive or physical device with a read-only viewing option. This opens the image as a drive and allows you to browse the content in Windows and other applications. The types supported are RAW/dd images, E01, S01, AFF, AD1, and L01. Full disk images are RAW/dd, E01, and S01, and these can be mounted physically, simulating a physical disk connected to the computer.

This feature allows you to add the emulated physical disk to a virtual machine, as shown in the following screenshot:

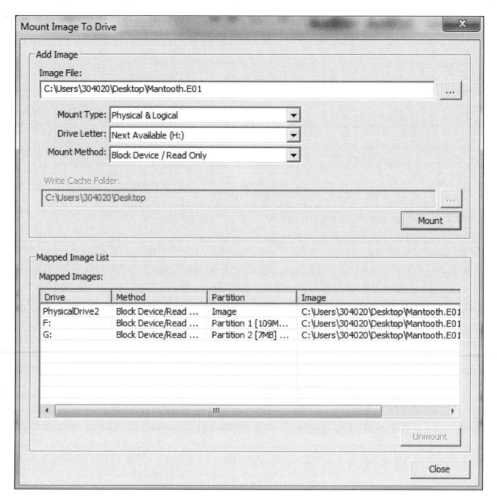

The Capture Memory feature

Volatile data, such as memory contents, has important evidence that must be analyzed.

Through the collection in the memory, you can extract information such as running processes, documents in use, websites accessed, username and password, and a lot more.

To execute the acquisition, perform the following steps:

1. Click on the **Memory Capture** button on the toolbar.

2. Select the destination path for the collected file.

3. As an optional step, you can include a `Pagefile.sys` file and create an AD1 evidence file format.

4. Click on **Capture Memory** to start the process as shown in the

5. following screenshot:

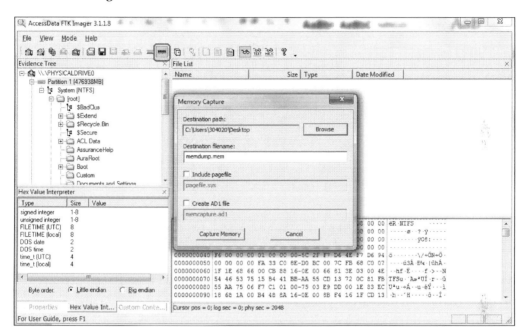

Obtaining the protected files

The Windows operating system does not allow you to copy or save live `Registry` files. You can acquire these protected registers running FTK Imager on the machine, which contains the records you want to copy as follows:

1. Click on the **Obtain Protected Files** button on the toolbar.

2. Select the destination folder for the obtained files.

3. Choose between the options of acquisition that are either needed to recover the password or the entire registry.

4. Click on **OK**, as shown in the following screenshot:

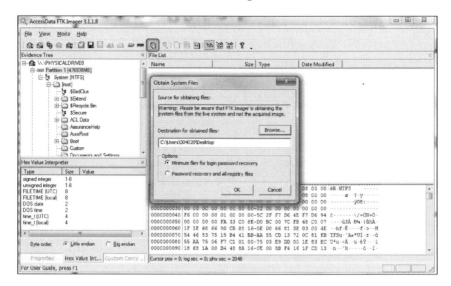

Detecting the EFS encryption

You can check for encrypted data on a physical drive or an image with FTK Imager just by clicking on the **Detect Encryption** button on the toolbar. The program scans the evidence and notifies you if the encrypted files have been located:

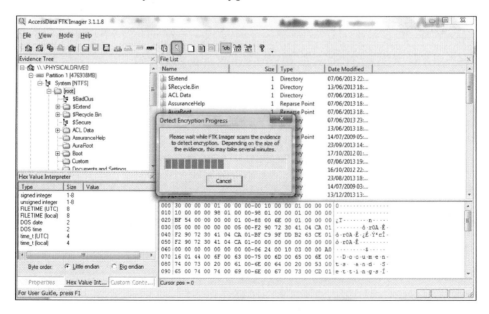

Summary

This chapter covered the main features of FTK Imager.

FTK Imager is a very important tool to produce forensic images and can support almost all evidence file formats. You can preview the evidence before the image. This is important because you can do a triage and collect only important information, considerably reducing the collection and analysis time.

You are able to understand the importance of using a write block device along with FTK Imager. In this way, it is possible to assure the integrity of a piece of evidence. You have learned about the interface in the solution and the main features of FTK Imager, as **Add and Preview Evidence Item**, **Creating Forensic Images**, **Image Mounting**, **Capture Memory**, **Obtain Protected Files**, and **Detect EFS Encryption**.

To summarize, FTK Imager is an essential tool for all experts and examiners. The best part of it is that it is free!

3
Working with Registry View

The AccessData Registry Viewer is a standalone product that can be integrated with the FTK and allows you to view the contents of the Windows registry. Unlike the traditional Windows Registry Editor, Regedit, which displays only the current system registry, the Registry Viewer can visualize registry files from any system. It also provides access to a registry-protected storage that contains passwords, usernames, and other information that is not accessible with Regedit. However, this tool is not free. In order to use it, you will need a CodeMeter USB stick with a valid license.

In this chapter, you will understand the structure of the Windows registry files, the main features of the tool, and its integration with the forensics FTK.

You'll see how to quickly access information from the users of the operating system, such as the following:

- Username
- Logon count
- Last logon time
- Last password change time
- Invalid logon time
- Last failed logon time

Understanding the Windows registry structure

To view the contents of the Windows registry keys, we need to identify the files associated with each key. These files are located at C:\Windows\System32\Config. The path and files are shown in the following screenshot:

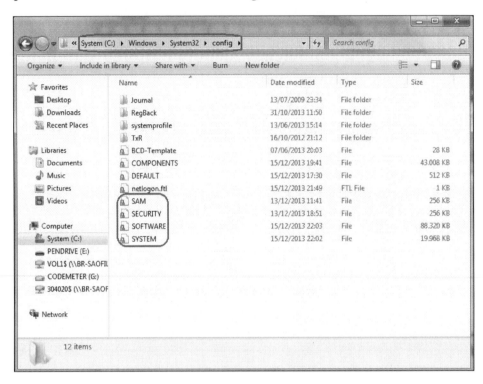

Another important key is located in each user folder and is called NTUSER.DAT. The location of this file is shown in the following screenshot:

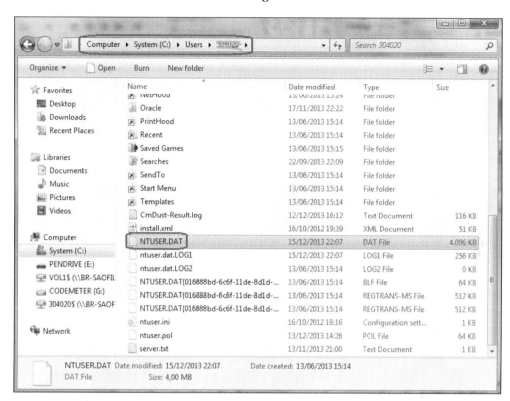

The main feature of Registry Viewer

The first step in setting up the Registry Viewer is to add one or more of the registry files previously presented in the Registry Viewer.

This can be done by performing the following steps:

1. Click on **Open** in the toolbar.

2. Select the registry file and click on **Open**:

The tool will interpret the data of the registry key and will present it in a friendly format, as shown in the following screenshot:

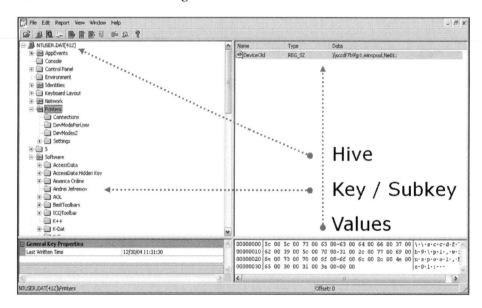

Generating a report

You can select important keys and add them to a report by performing the following steps:

1. Select the key you would like to add to the report and right-click on it.

2. Click on **Add to Report**.

3. To generate the report, click on the **Report** option in the toolbar.

4. Click on **OK**:

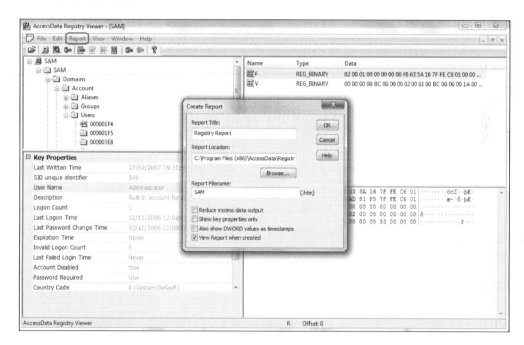

Integrating with FTK

There are two different ways to manipulate the files of the registry keys. To access these files, you can use FTK Imager to locate and export these files.

The following screenshot shows a sample of this export process:

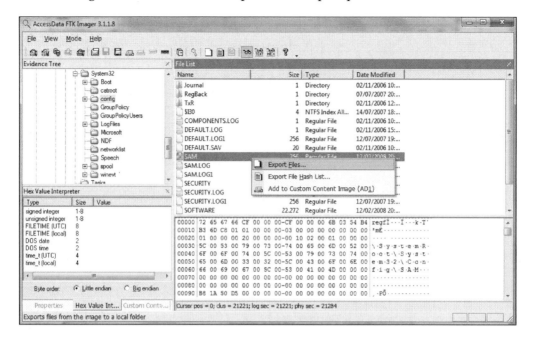

Alternatively, you can use the FTK to export the same files, as shown in the following screenshot. You can do this by right-clicking on the registry file and then clicking on **Open in Registry Viewer**.

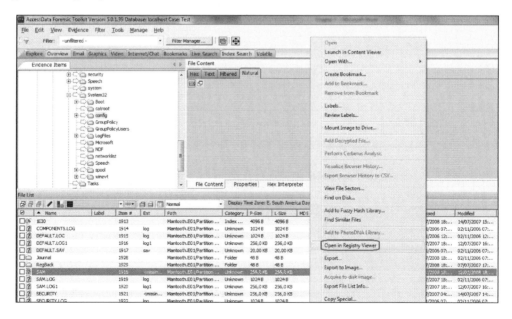

Identifying the Time Zone setting

The correct setting of the time zone is critical for proper analysis and generation of the results of the investigation process; incorrect settings may result in erroneous claims about those facts. When you select the correct **Time Zone**, all MAC time information is adjusted automatically as follows:

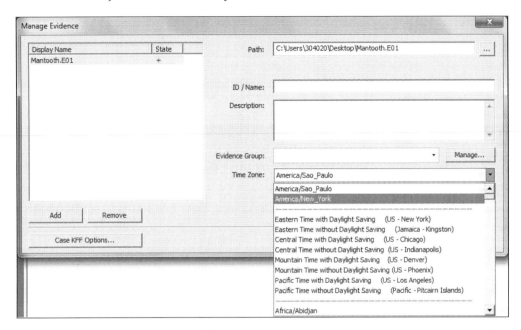

If you do not know the time zone of the seized computer, Registry Viewer can help you.

You can add the registry key, System, and locate the information at `System\ControlSet001\Control\TimeZoneInformation,` as shown in the following screenshot:

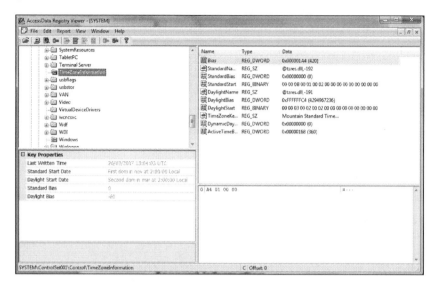

Account information

Another important feature of the Registry Viewer is the ability to view information about all the users of the system in a very easy way. This important information is shown in the following screenshot:

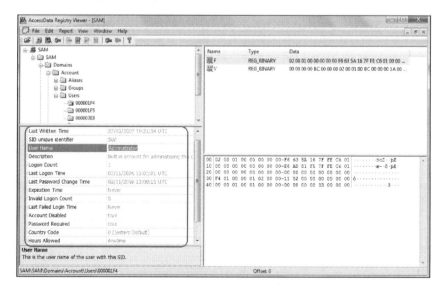

Summary

This chapter covered the use of the Registry Viewer, which is presented in its interface and main features. You are now able to understand the importance of the correct use of the **Time Zone** feature and how to locate it within Windows registry keys. The Registry Viewer can display key bits of information about the user accounts in a friendly manner. It is certainly an important tool for conducting research on registry information that cannot be accessed by the operating system. It is easy to use and very useful during the investigation process because it allows you to quickly access information contained in the registry keys and helps to interpret their values.

In the next chapter, you will learn how to manage their investigation cases and the options for processing evidence, which is one of the most important tasks of the FTK.

Working with FTK Forensics

4

As mentioned in previous chapters, the FTK is a complete platform for digital investigations, and although it has a friendly interface, its use requires attention, especially during the preanalysis phase. A wrong setting of the case can generate negative impacts on the project and may require more time than planned.

This chapter will cover the process of computer forensics and the first steps of using the FTK.

You will notice that the correct understanding of the computer forensics process will help you with the use of the tool, and the right the FTK setup will save you a lot of analysis time and provide you with the best results.

Introducing computer forensics and FTK

Computer forensics is a digital forensic science that relates to the generation of legal evidence found in computers and the digital media. The computer forensics process aims at examining the digital media in a forensically sound manner with the goal of acquiring, preserving, analyzing, and presenting relevant facts about a specific case; for example, digital crime, fraud, misuse of resources, and so on.

The steps presented in the following diagram are intended to help drive the research process and get the evidence that could be presented in court, demonstrating that the best practices of computer forensics were followed. The computer forensics process can be explained using the steps shown in the following diagram:

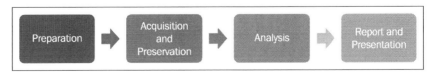

Preparation

It is very important for the forensic analyst to be prepared to start a new digital investigation process and should take care of with the following points:

- Defined investigation processes are required
- A trained field and lab team that must include the following:
    - **Technical trainings**: This is done to know how to use the main computer forensics tools
    - **Procedural trainings**: This is done to understand the best practices, procedures, and flows to conduct a digital investigation
- Adequate software and hardware

Acquisition and preservation

Acquisition and preservation are considered as the most critical steps of the process since errors are not allowed at the time of evidence acquisition. The basic principle of computer forensics is preservation of the digital evidence integrity.

The acquisition can be done using the following tools:

- Write blockers (hardware or software)
- Forensic duplicators
- Boot disks
- Remote acquisition (through network)

Analysis

Analysis is the part of the investigation process that involves the most amount of technical aspects. Some of the reasons are listed as follows:

- Necessary technical knowledge about operation system, filesystem, network, and applications
- Specialized software is required
- Skill for creating filters and searching evidence in operational systems artifacts

Reports and presentation

This is the last step of the process. After we have found results and arrived at conclusions about the investigation, we need to perform the following steps:

- Adapt the report language for the target audience—use technical language for the technical team or more formal and appropriate language for lawyers or judges

- Take care that the reports and presentations are clear and conclusive and avoid opinions

- Provide the presentation in different kinds of file formats such as PDF, HTML, DOC, and so on

Managing groups and users

The FTK allows you to create multiple users and assign roles to them, providing a more collaborative solution.

To add a new user, we have to perform the following steps:

1. Click on **Database** and select **Administer Users**.

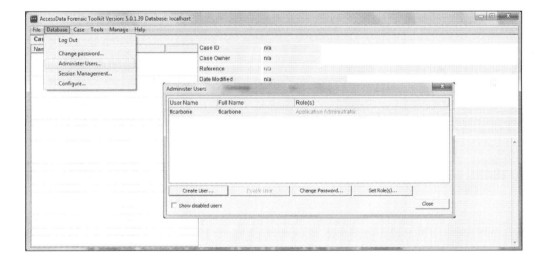

2. Click on the **Create User...** button.

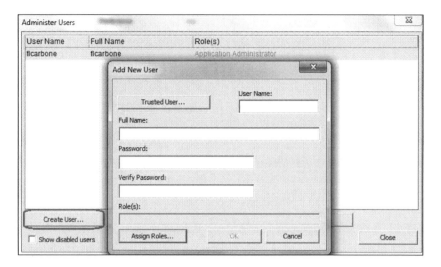

3. Fill in the presented fields as follows:

   ○ **User Name**: In this field, enter the name that will be recognized by the FTK

   ○ **Full Name**: In this field, enter the full name that should appear on case reports

   ○ **Password**: In this field, enter the password for the user

   ○ **Verify Password**: In this field, enter the same password for verification

4. After entering the required information into the fields, click on **Assign Roles**.

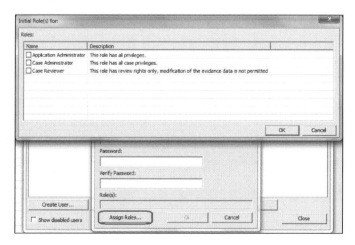

5. To assign rights to this user, use one of the roles presented as follows:

   ○ **Application Administrator**: This performs all tasks, including adding and managing users

   ○ **Case Administrator**: This performs all tasks that an application administrator can perform, except creating and managing users

   ○ **Case Reviewer**: This cannot create cases; it only processes cases

6. After choosing the correct profile, click on **OK** to apply the role, and then click on **OK** again to create the user.

The user's passwords can be changed at any time. Just click on **Change Password...** to enter the new password, as shown in the following screenshot:

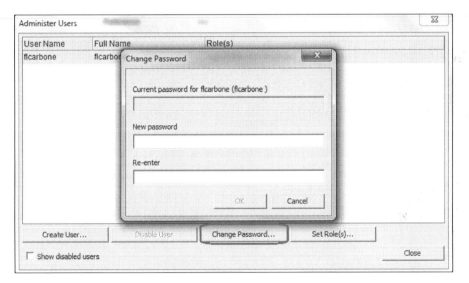

Creating a new investigation case

The FTK allows you to manage your investigations by assigning a case for each of them. The case information is stored in a database.

To create a new case, perform the following steps:

1. Click on **New...** and select **New Case**. The **New Case Options** dialog opens, as shown in the following screenshot:

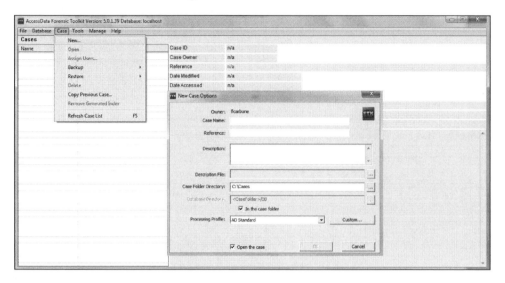

2. Fill in the fields that appear in the following manner:
    ○   **Case Name**: In this field, enter the name of the case.
    ○   **Description**: This field is optional and text free.
    ○   **Reference**: This field is also optional and text free.
    ○   **Description File**: In this field, you can attach a file to the case.
    ○   **Case Folder Directory**: This holds the path where case files will be stored.
    ○   **Database Directory**: This is the path where case database will be stored. Select the **In the case folder** checkbox to set the same folder of the case.
    ○   **Processing Profile**: Configure the default processing options for the case by either using a processing profile or custom settings. This item will be detailed in the next topic.
    ○   **Open the case**: Check this option if you wish to open the case as soon as it is created. After the fields are filled, click on **OK** to create the new case.

3. The next step is to add the evidence file, as shown in the following screenshot:

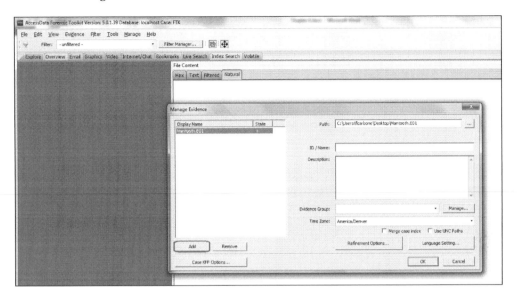

4. Click on **Add** and select one of the following evidence types:

   ° **Acquired Image(s)**: Select this type to add an image file (dd, e01, AD1, and so on)

   ° **All Images in Directory**: Select this to add all images in a specific folder

   ° **Contents of a Directory**: Select this type to add all files in a specific folder

   ° **Individual File(s)**: Select this to add a single file (docx, pdf, jpg, and so on)

   ° **Physical Drive**: Select this to add a physical device (a full hard disk)

   ° **Logical Drive**: Select this to add a logical volume or partition, for example, the C or D drive

5. Click on **OK** set the following items:

   ° **Time Zone**: Select the correct time zone of the location where the evidence was collected.

   ° **Refinement Options**: Select which items will be processed in evidence. This item will be detailed in the next topic.

   ° **Language Settings**: Select the correct language that corresponds to the alphabet used in the collected evidence.

6. Once all the parameters are configured, click on **OK** and wait for the evidence processing.

 Incorrect use of the **Time Zone** option can produce inconsistent results because it changes all MAC time values of evidence. If you do not know the **Time Zone** option of the evidence, use the FTK registry viewer tool to identify it.

The FTK interface

The main feature of the FTK interface is the location, organization, and exportation of data. The interface contains tabs, each with a specific focus, and also contains a common toolbar and file list with customizable columns. New tabs can be added to help the localization of information as shown in the following screenshot:

The tabs can be categorized as follows:

- **Menus/Toolbar**: In this option, all the functionalities and settings of the tools can be accessed. Use filters to find relevant evidence.

- **Tabs**: Each tab will display the data in different structures as follows:

  ○ **Explorer**: This tab lists the evidence in a directory structure, similar to the Windows explorer. Evidence can be viewed in physical or logical drives.

- ° **Overview**: This tab narrows your search to look through specific document types or to look for items by the status or file extension.

- ° **Email**: This tab is used to view e-mails, mailboxes, and attachments.

- ° **Graphics**: This tab gives a quick view of the case graphics through thumbnails.

- ° **Video**: This tab is used to watch video contents and the detailed information about them. It is possible to create thumbnails from videos files.

- ° **Internet/Chat**: This tab is used to view detailed information about the Internet artifact data in your case.

- ° **Bookmarks**: This tab generates a group of files to be referenced in the case. All relevant information found during the investigation can be placed on the bookmark for the generation of reports.

- ° **Live Search**: This tab is used to search information in the case using keywords. This type of search processes the results slower as it involves a bit-by-bit comparison of the used keyword against the evidence.

- ° **Index Search**: As the data was previously indexed in the processing phase, in this tab the results will be provided quicker.

- ° **Volatile**: In this tab you can view and analyze data collected from volatile sources such as memory.

- **Evidence tree viewer**: This viewer presents the data structure, depending on the selections made in the tabs.

- **File list viewer**: This viewer displays case files and pertinent information about files, such as filename, file path, file type, and many others properties. The **File List** view reflects the files of the selected folder in the explorer tab.

- **File content viewer**: This viewer displays the content of the currently selected file from the **File List** view. The **Viewer** toolbar gives you the choice of different view formats.

Case processing options

To work better with your investigation case, the evidence data should be processed. When evidence is processed, data about the evidence is created and stored in the database. The processed data can be viewed at any time.

If you want to process the evidence as quickly as possible, you can use a predefined field mode that deselects almost all processing options. If you need an item for later, an additional analysis can be performed to enable additional processing options. Or, if you have time to categorize and index files, more options can be enabled. This step will take a significant amount of time for a large evidence set. Take a look at the options shown in the following screenshot:

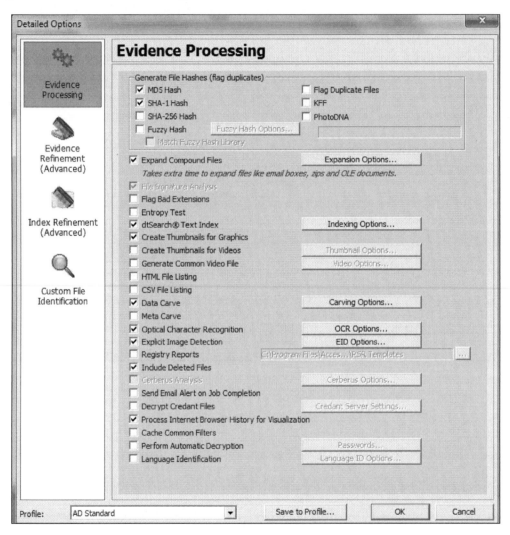

The following table presents a brief explanation of each item:

Options	Description
MD5 Hash	Creates a digital fingerprint using MD5
SHA-1 Hash	Creates a digital fingerprint using SHA-1
SHA-256 Hash	Creates a digital fingerprint using SHA-256
Fuzzy Hash	Compares hash values to determine the similar data
Match Fuzzy Hash Library	Matches new evidence against the Fuzzy hash library
Flag Duplicate Files	Identifies files that are found more than once in the evidence
KFF	Uses a database of hashes from known files
PhotoDNA	Compares images in your evidence against known images in a library
Expand Compound Files	Mounts and processes the contents of compound files such as ZIP, e-mails, and OLE files
File Signature Analysis	Analyzes files to indicate whether their headers match their extensions
Flag Bad Extensions	Identifies files whose types do not match their extensions
Entropy Test	Finds compressed or encrypted files
dtSearch Text Index	Indexes the case for a quick retrieval of the keyword search
Create Thumbnails for Graphics	Creates thumbnails for all the graphics in a case
Create Thumbnails for Videos	Creates thumbnails for all the videos in a case
Generate Common Video File	Creates a common video type for the videos in your case
HTML File Listing	Creates an HTML version of the File listing in the case folder
CSV File Listing	Creates a CSV version of the File Listing in the case folder
Data Carve	Identifies deleted files in the evidence based on file signatures
Meta Carve	Locates deleted directory entries and other metadata

Options	Description
Optical Character Recognition (OCR)	Extracts text from graphics files to be recognized during a keyword process
Explicit Image Detection	Identifies suspect explicit content
Registry Reports	Creates **Registry Summary Reports (RSR)** from case content automatically
Include Deleted Files	Shows deleted files in the case
Cerberus Analysis	Runs the Cerberus Malware Triage module
Send Email Alert on Job Completion	Sends a message once a job is completed when an e-mail address is inserted in this field
Decrypt Credant Files	Locates and decrypts files encrypted by the Credant solution
Process Internet Browser History for Visualization	Processes Internet browser history files to be seen in the detailed visualization timeline
Cache Common Filters	Caches commonly viewed files in the list of files
Perform Automatic Decryption	Attempts to decrypt files using a list of passwords provided by you
Language Identification	Automatically attempts to identify the evidence language

The last option, located on the bottom the screen, is **Profile**. It is possible to use the default profiles or create a customized one.

These options can be changed or added later just by clicking on the **Evidence** option in the toolbar and selecting **Additional Analysis**.

 It is important that you select only the necessary items for your case investigation because the selection of many items can greatly increase processing time.

Refining the case evidence

The evidence refinement process allows the specification of how the evidence is sorted and displayed, by adding or removing data according to date filters, file types, and status.

To set case evidence refining options, perform the following steps:

1. Click on the **Evidence Refinement (Advanced)** icon in the left-hand side pane. The following two dialog tabs will be seen:

    ° **Refine Evidence by File Status/Type**

    ° **Refine Evidence by File Date/Size**

2. Click on the corresponding tab as shown in the following screenshot:

This first tab allows you to focus on specific files needed for a case, including or removing files by type or status. For example, if you only search for evidence in Word files, it is much more effective if you apply the filters and only select the **Documents** checkbox in the **File Types** list as shown in the following screenshot:

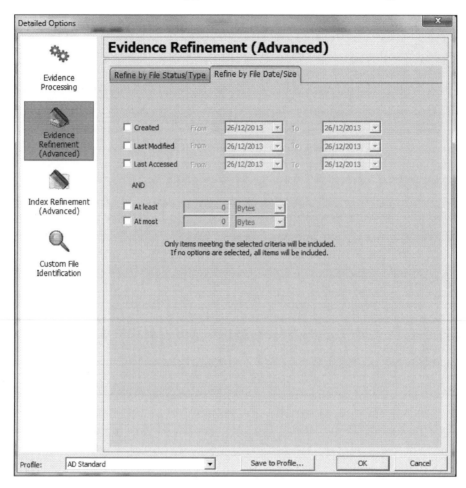

The second tab refines evidence by the date range or file size. In a scenario where you already know some information about the data you are seeking, it is recommended to apply this filter. A lot of processing time is saved.

The **Index Refinement (Advanced)** feature is very similar to the **Evidence Refinement (Advanced)** feature and allows you to specify types of data that you do not want to index. Use it to exclude data to save time or increase searching efficiency.

Summary

This chapter covered the overview of the computer forensics process, showing its importance during the process of research and how it can help your organization with your case investigation. You were presented with the FTK interface, which will be worked out in detail in the next chapter. It also covered one of the most important processes used in the FTK tool; the processing options case. If configured correctly, it can improve processing time and the results of the analysis considerably.

In the next chapter, we will delve into the subject of processing and analyzing the artifacts using the FTK operating system and other advanced features of the tool.

5
Processing the Case

This chapter will cover how to use the most important features for processing and filtering data during an investigation process.

The processing step is considered to be the most important step because the correct utilization of its functionality can be decisive in the relevant results of an investigation.

You will understand the importance of the correct use of the Time Zone feature and how this impacts the properties of the files, and learn how to use filters and searches. Finally, you will be able to generate a report of your findings.

Changing the time zone

The correct use of the **Time Zone** feature is of the utmost importance for computer forensics because it might reflect the wrong MAC time of files contained in the evidence, making a professional use the wrong information in an investigation report.

Based on this, you must configure the time zone to reflect the location where the evidence was acquired. For example, if you conducted the acquisition of a computer that was located in Los Angeles, US, and bring the evidence to Sao Paulo, Brazil, where your lab is situated, you should adjust the time zone to Los Angeles so that the MAC time of files can reflect the actual moment of its modification, alteration, or creation.

The FTK allows you to make that time zone change at the same time that you add a new evidence to the case. Select the time zone of the evidence where it was seized from the drop-down list in the **Time Zone** field. This is required to add evidence in the case.

Take a look at the following screenshot:

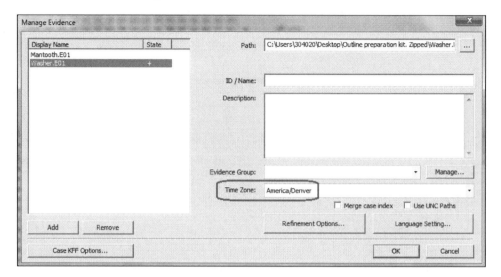

 You can also change the value of **Time Zone** after adding the evidence. In the menu toolbar, click on **View** and then click on **Time Zone Display**.

Mounting compound files

To locate important information during your investigation, you should expand individual compound file types. This lets you see the child files that are contained within a container, such as ZIP or RAR files. You can access this feature from the case manager's new case wizard, or from the **Add Evidence** or **Additional Analysis** dialogs.

The following are some of the compound files that you can mount:

- **E-mail files**: PST, NSF, DBX, and MSG
- **Compressed files**: ZIP, RAR, GZIP, TAR, BZIP, and 7-ZIP
- **System files**: Windows thumbnails, registry, PKCS7, MS Office, and EVT

 If you don't mount compound files, the child files will not be located in keyword searches or filters.

To expand compound files, perform the following steps:

1. Do one of the following:
   ° For new cases, click on the **Custom** button in the **New Case Options** dialog
   ° For existing cases, go to **Evidence | Additional Analysis**

2. Select **Expand Compound Files**.

3. Click on **Expansion Options...**.

4. In the **Compound File Expansions Options** dialog, select the types of files that you want to mount.

5. Click on **OK**:

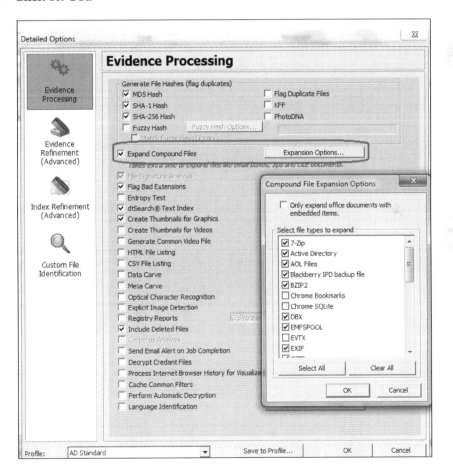

File and folder export

You may need to export part of the files or folders to help you perform some action outside of the FTK platform, or simply for the evidence presentation.

To export files or folders you need to perform the following steps:

1. Select one or more files that you would like to export.

2. Right-click on the selection and select **Export**.

3. A new dialog will open. You can configure some settings before exporting as follows:

    ◦ **File Options**: This field has advanced options to export files and folders. You can use the default options for a simple export.

    ◦ **Items to Include**: This field has the selection of files and folders that you will export. The options can be checked, listed, highlighted, or selected all together.

    ◦ **Destination base path**: This field has the folder to save the files.

    Take a look at the following screenshot:

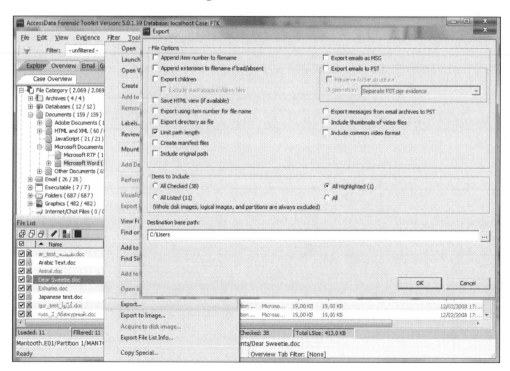

Column settings

Columns are responsible for presenting the information property or metadata related to evidence data. By default, the FTK presents the most commonly used columns. However, you can add or remove columns to aid you in quickly finding relevant information. To manage columns in FTK, in the **File List** view, right-click on column bars and select **Column Settings....**The number of columns available is huge. You can add or remove the columns that you need by just selecting the type and clicking on the **Add** button:

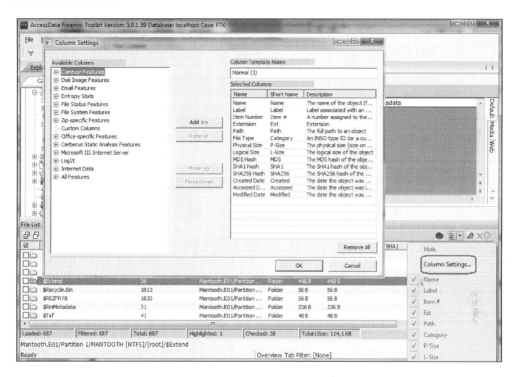

The FTK has some templates of columns settings. You can access them by clicking on **Manage** and navigating to **Columns | Manage Columns**:

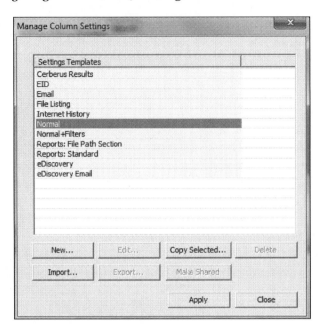

You can use some ready-made templates, edit them, or create your own.

Creating and managing bookmarks

A bookmark is a group of files that you want to reference in your case. These are user-created groups and the list is stored for later reference and for use in the report output. You can create as many bookmarks as needed in a case. Bookmarks can be nested within other bookmarks for convenience and categorization purposes. Bookmarks help organize the case evidence by grouping related or similar files. For example, you can create a bookmark of graphics that contain similar or related graphic images. The **Bookmarks** tab lists all bookmarks that have been created in the current case.

To create a bookmark, perform the following steps:

1. In the **File List** view, select the files that you want to add to the bookmark.
2. Right-click on selected files and click on **Create Bookmark**.
3. Enter the information about the bookmark.
4. Click on **OK**:

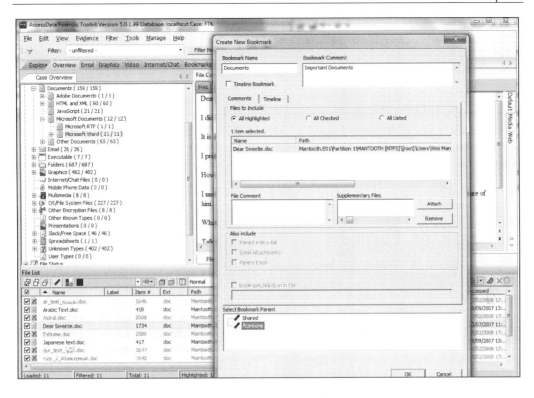

The main options to create new bookmarks are as follows:

- **Bookmark Name**: This is the name of your new bookmark.

- **Bookmark Comment**: This option includes free text regarding your bookmark.

- **Timeline Bookmark**: Select this option to create a timeline bookmark. This option shows the chronological relationships of the files in your case.

- **File to Include**: With this option, you can see the files that you had selected earlier.

- **File Comment**: This option includes free text about your file.

- **Supplementary Files**: With this option, you can attach external files that can help in your investigation case.

- **Also include**: In this option, you can include **Parent index.dat**, **Email Attachments**, and **Parent Email** if applicable.

- **Select Bookmark Parent**: This is the folder that you will use to create the bookmark, and it will determine if the bookmark will be private or shared.

Once the bookmark is created, you can add or remove files when necessary.

 You can bookmark other information such as selected text, e-mails, and e-mail attachments.

The Additional Analysis feature

After the evidence has been added to a case and processed, you may wish to perform other analysis tasks. To further analyze the selected evidence, click on **Evidence** and then click on **Additional Analysis**.

Most of the tasks available during the initial evidence processing remain available with **Additional Analysis**. You can perform multiple processing tasks at the same time. Make your selections and click on **OK** to create a new job, as shown in the following screenshot:

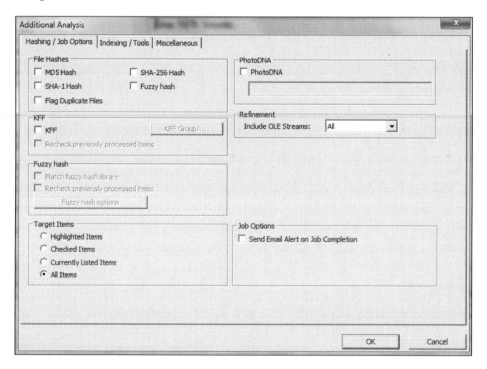

The explanation of all the processing options has been detailed previously. Refer to *Chapter 4, Working with FTK Forensics*.

Carving the data

Data carving is the process of looking for data in the evidence that was deleted from the filesystem. This is done by identifying file headers and footers in mainly unallocated clusters. The FTK provides several predefined carvers that you can select when adding evidence to a case. You can also create your own custom carvers to meet your exact needs.

Data carving can be selected in the **New Case Wizard** or later, using the **Additional Analysis** feature:

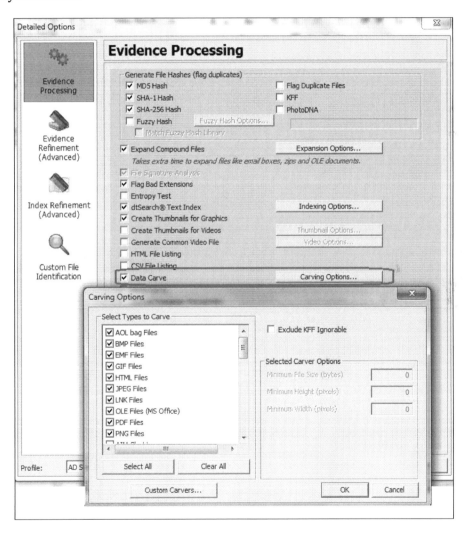

In the **Carving Options** dialog box, you can select the file types that you want to try to recover and click on **OK** to go back to **Detailed Options** to then perform the task.

You can also create your own carvers, informing the header and footers of the files that you would like to recover. To create the carver, perform the following steps:

1. In the toolbar menu, click on **Manage**.
2. Click on the **Carvers** option
3. Next, select **Manage Custom Carvers**.

After the carver is processed, you can find the carved files using the **Carved Files** filter or through the following steps:

1. Change the view to the **Overview** tab.
2. Select the **File Status** option.
3. Finally, click on **Data Carved Files**.

Narrowing the case with KFF

The **Known File Filter (KFF)** is a database utility that compares known filehash values against your case files.

Using the KFF during your analysis, we can do the following:

* Immediately identify and ignore 40 to 70 percent of files
* Immediately identify known contraband files

 A hash is based on data and not names or extensions.

The KFF database is based on NSRL from **National Institute of Standards and Technology (NIST)** and can be downloaded from the AccessData website at http://www.accessdata.com/support/product-downloads.

The KFF can be selected in the **New Case Wizard** or later, using the **Additional Analysis** feature.

To import a new KFF database and define a group, perform the following steps:

1. Click on **Manage** and select **KFF**.
2. Click on **Import** to select a new database.

3. To locate a database file, click on **Add File**.

4. Select the **Status**: **Alert** or **Ignore**.

5. Insert the path where file is located.

6. Click on **OK** to go back to **KFF Hash Import Tool**.

7. Click on **Import** to process your new KFF database.

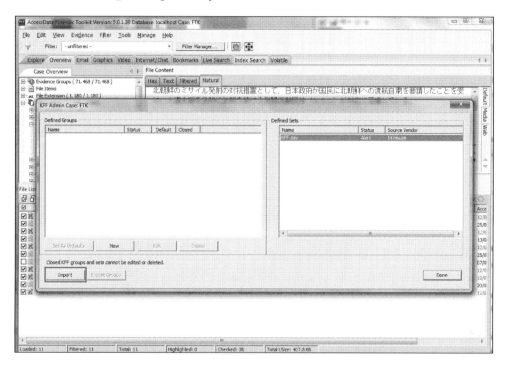

8. In **KFF Admin Case**, click on **New** to create a group.

9. Add the KFF database processed previously.

10. Click on **Done** to finish.

To run the KFF in your case, open the **Additional Analysis** options:

1. Select **KFF** and click on **KFF Groups…**.

2. Check the name of the group created previously.

3. Click on **Done**.

4. Finally, click on **OK** to start new job.

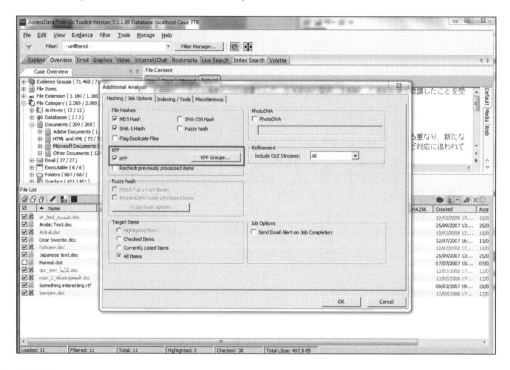

To use the results of the KFF to hide a known file from your case, use the following filters:

- **KFF Alert Files**
- **KFF Ignore Files**

Searching the case

One of the most important features of the tool, the search keyword, is used in almost all cases of research and can help you locate relevant information contained in files, documents, and e-mails.

The Index Search and Live Search options

A live search is a bit-by-bit comparison of the entire evidence set with the search term and takes slightly more time than an index search. Live searches also allow you to search regular expressions and hex values.

To conduct a live search, you can perform the following steps:

1. Click on the **Live Search** tab.

2. In the **Text** tab, insert your keyword and click on **Add**.

3. You will now see the keyword inserted in the **Search Terms** list; click on **Search**.

4. The results will appear in **Live Search Results** with the numbers of hits:

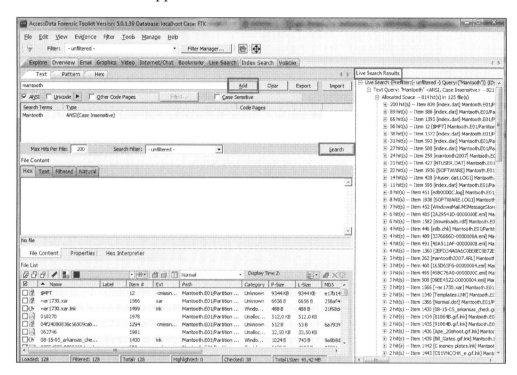

The **Index Search** option compares search terms with the indexed database. You should choose to generate an index file during preprocessing to use this kind of search.

To perform an index search, you can perform the following steps:

1. Click on the **Index Search** tab.

2. In the **Terms** section, insert your keyword and click on **Add**.

3. The possible hits of your keyword will be displayed immediately. Select the most appropriate and double-click on it.

4. You will see the keyword inserted in the **Search Terms** list; click on **Search Now**.

5. The results will appear in **Index Search Results** with the numbers of hits:

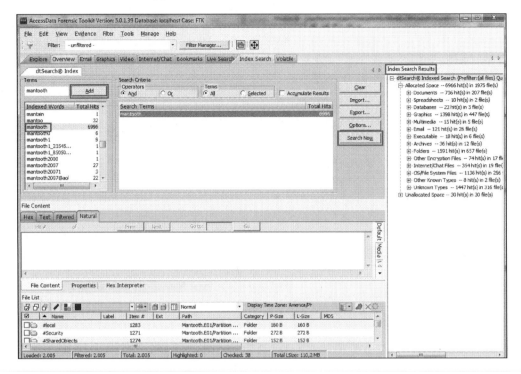

Regular expressions

A **regular expression (regex)** is a special text string used for describing a search pattern and can help identify information that has some predefined pattern, such as a phone number or credit card. The following screenshot shows such search patterns:

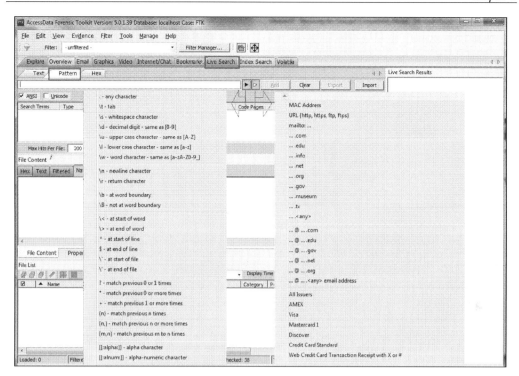

As you can see, the FTK has a huge list of ready-to-use regular expressions. However, you can create your own regular expressions to better achieve your goals.

Regular expressions are complex to construct. To understand better the techniques for building regular expressions, you can consult other sources such as Wikipedia at `http://en.wikipedia.org/wiki/Regular_expression`.

Working with filters

Filters can help to locate specific data very quickly, reducing the amount of time spent on examining data, because they can narrow a large data set down to a very specific focus.

You can use the predefined filters or you can create your own filters. To use predefined filters, just click on the combobox in the **Filter** toolbar as shown in the following screenshot:

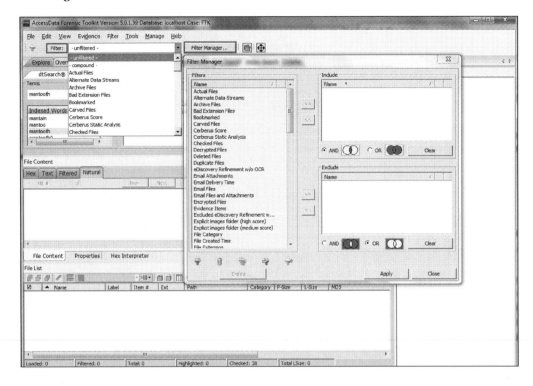

You also can make a combination between filters. Click on **Filter Manager...** to create your combinations.

To create a new filter, perform the following steps:

1. Click on **Manage** and navigate to **Filters | Manager Filters**.

2. Click on **New**.

3. Enter a name and a description for the new filter.

4. Select properties from the drop-down menu.

5. Select operators from the drop-down menu.

6. Select the applicable criteria from the drop-down menu.

7. Click on the **+** button to add new item in the rules.

8. Select the **Match Any** option to use the OR operator or the **Match All** option to use the AND operator.

9. To test a filter without having to save it first, check the **Live Preview** box.

10. Click on **Save** and then click on **Close**.

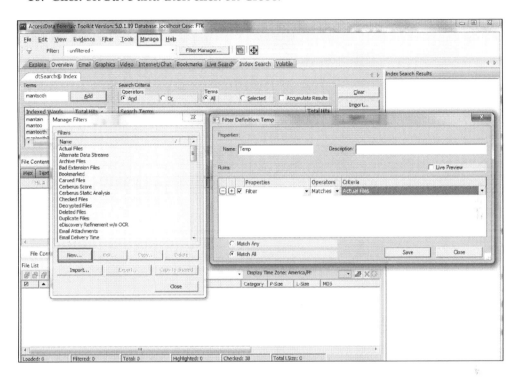

Reporting the case

The report is the most important part of your process. This is what is seen of the work by recipients. All the analysis work is useless if the report cannot clearly show the links between the identified evidence and the alleged offence.

You can create a case report about the relevant information of your investigation case. Reports can be generated in different formats, including HTML and PDF.

To create a case report, perform the following steps:

1. Click on **File** and then click on **Report...** to run the **Report** wizard:

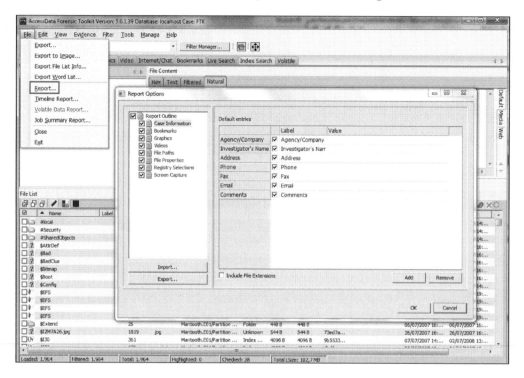

2. Select the information that will be used for the generation of the report in the **Report Outline** box and fill the information related to each.

3. Click on **OK**:

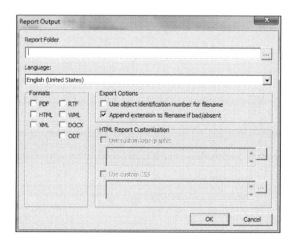

4. In the **Report Folder** field, set the path to output your report.

5. Select a language to use on report.

6. Select the output file format.

7. Click on **OK** to generate a final report.

You can distribute your report in a printed form by e-mail, portable media, or as a website.

Summary

This chapter covered several important features to assist in the identification of relevant information quickly and efficiently through the use of filters and keywords. The use of the KFF and how its features can be useful to save time during an investigation by eliminating the known files of your investigation case was covered. The creation and management of bookmarks and how you can generate a final report using this information was also covered.

In the next chapter, you will learn about the new features of FTK v5.

6
New Features of FTK 5

This chapter is an overview of the main new features that have been developed in the newest version of the product, the FTK 5.

We will not explore all features in detail, but you will be able to understand the goals of each one of them and apply them in your investigation case.

Let's understand how these new features can help us to locate evidence quickly; a task that would earlier have taken a long time or may even have been impossible to achieve without a specific tool.

Distributed processing

Distributed processing allows you to improve performance and process investigation cases using computational resources of other computers on your network.

To use this resource, you need to install the **Distributed Processing Engine** (DPE) add-on in all the additional computers that you have available.

We know that the processing step requires a lot of hardware resources and the distributed processing can help us to reduce processing time without having to perform an upgrade on the examiner machine.

The DPE product can be found on the FTK installation disk in the path
`[Drive]:\FTK\AccessData Distributed Processing Engine.EXE`.

Once the DPE is installed, you can use other machines to process your case, load balancing, and minimizing the processing time.

Encryption support

FTK users can send files directly to **Password Recovery Toolkit (PRTK)** for on-the-fly password recovery during evidence review.

Files supported include: Credant, SafeBoot, Utimaco, SafeGuard Enterprise and Easy, EFS, PGP, GuardianEdge, Pointsec, S/MIME OpenOffice, TrueCrypt, FileVault (Apple), FileVault 2 (Apple), DMG files (Apple), RAR, ZIP including WinZip advanced encryption, 7-Zip, password protected iOS backup files, PGP password files, BCArchive, BCTextEncoder, ABICoder, AdvancedFileLock, AShampoo, CryptoForge, Cypherus, and more.

The PRTK tool will be presented in detail in the next chapter.

Data visualization

Data visualization is a feature that provides a graphical interface to enhance understanding and analysis of the files and e-mails in a case. You view data based on the file and e-mail dates.

Data visualization supports the following data types:

- **File data**: This lets you view file data from either the **Explore** tab or the **Overview** tab
- **E-mail data**: This lets you view e-mail data from the **Email** tab
- **Internet browser history**: This lets you view Internet browser history data

To open data visualization, see the **Explorer**, **Overview**, or **Email** tab to select your dataset. Click on **Tools** and select **Visualization**.

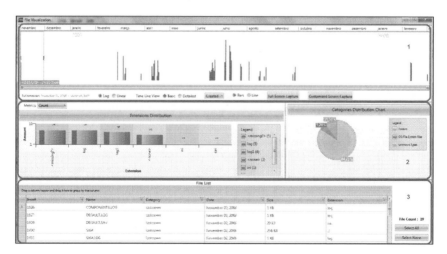

Data visualization has the following three main components:

- **Time line pane**: This provides graphics that represent the available data
- **Dashboard**: This provides graphical chart panes of the data
- **Data list pane**: This provides a list of the data items

 Normally, to use the data visualization feature, you need a separate license. Check this information at the time of acquisition of the solution.

The Single-node enterprise

As mentioned in *Chapter 1*, *Getting Started with Computer Forensics Using FTK*, to conduct a remote acquisition through the network, you need a product in the enterprise version, such as the AD of AccessData Enterprise.

However, a very interesting feature of FTK forensics is that it allows this remote acquisition limited to a single agent called Single-node enterprise. To use this feature, perform the following steps:

1. Click on **Tools** and select **Push Agents**.
2. Insert the IP address or hostname of the machine that you want to acquire and click on **Add**.
3. Click on **OK**.

4. Insert the credentials information of the remote machine or of your active directory structure and click on **Add**.

5. Click on **OK** to start the deploy agent process.

You may also run the agent manually. It is located in the path `C:\Program Files\AccessData\Forensic Toolkit\5.0\bin\Agent`.

Once an agent is distributed to the remote machine, you can connect this device and perform a pre-analysis or data acquisition by performing the following steps:

1. Click on **Evidence** and then select **Add Remote Data**.

2. Insert the remote IP address and click on **OK**.

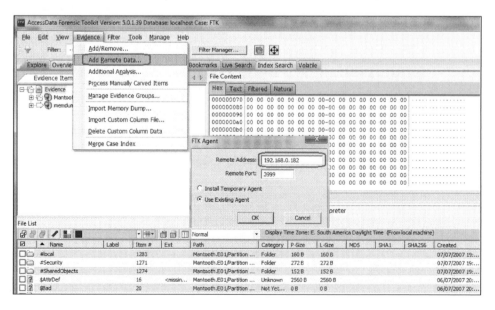

The machine will be added as an evidence allowing the analysis or acquisition process.

 Check if the TCP port 3999 (default port) is enabled on the firewall and if the WMI service is enabled and running.

Advanced volatile and memory analysis

Volatile data is information that changes frequently and is often lost upon powering down the computer. The acquisition of this type of information should be made with the equipment powered on, which is known as live acquisition.

Volatile data will include information about the running process, network connections, clipboard contents, and data in memory. This information may be critical to the discovery of the cause of an incident or to understand a specific behavior.

As seen in previous chapters, the FTK imager can help in the collection of this data, specifically memory acquisition. Once collected, you can do a deeper analysis using the platform FTK.

To start the memory analysis, firstly add the file of dump in your case as follows:

1. Click on **Evidence** and select **Import Memory Dump**.
2. Once added, select the **Volatile** tab to see all the extracted data of the evidence.

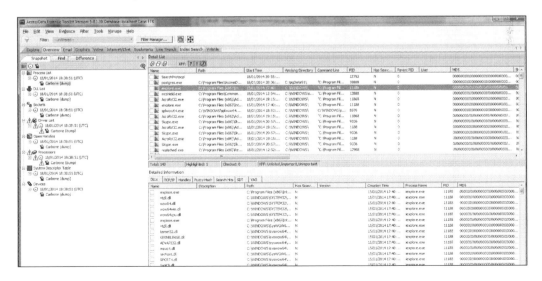

The information is presented in a classified and categorized form using a friendly FTK interface, to help the process of analysis.

Explicit Image Detection

If your investigation case has some relation with the search of explicit material, you can use **Explicit Image Detection (EID)** to locate this kind of content in evidence, thus avoiding a manual search of this information.

To execute EID analysis, perform the following steps:

1. Click on **Evidence** and select **Additional Analysis**.
2. Select the **Indexing/Tools** tab.
3. In the section **Other Tools**, select the **Explicit Image Detection** option.
4. Choose the tree scan type options and click on **OK**.

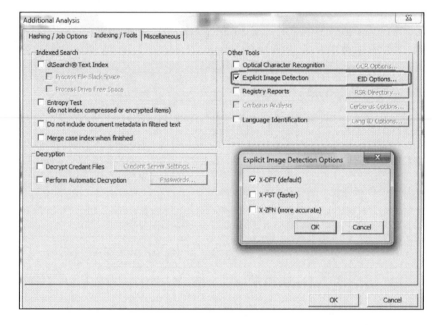

The difference between the types of scans is related to the accuracy of research, which may have an impact on the time to complete the process if you choose higher accuracy.

To visualize the results of the analysis of EID, just use the filters related to **Explicit Images Folder**.

Normally, to use the feature of EID, you need a separate license. Check this information at the time of acquisition of the solution.

Malware triage and analysis with Cerberus

Cerberus lets you do a malware analysis on executable binaries. You can use Cerberus to analyze executable binaries on a disk, on a network share, or unpacked in system memory.

Cerberus consists of the following stages of analysis:

- **Threat analysis**: This is general file and metadata analysis that identifies potentially malicious code
- **Static analysis**: This is disassembly analysis that examines elements of the code

To use Cerberus is very simple; just perform the following steps:

1. Click on **Evidence** and select **Additional Analysis**.
2. Select the **Indexing/Tools** tab.
3. In the section **Other Tools**, select the **Cerberus Analysis** option.

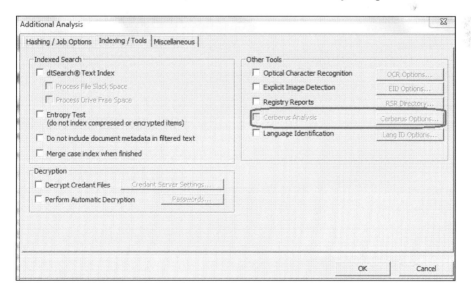

The results of the Cerberus analysis generates and assigns a threat score to the executable binary as seen in the following screenshot:

To visualize the results of the analysis of Cerberus, just use the filters related to **Cerberus Score** or **Cerberus Static Analysis**.

 Normally, to use the feature of Cerberus, you need a separate license. Check this information at the time of acquisition of the solution.

Mobile Phone Examiner

Smartphones have become one of the most important evidence to be analyzed during an investigation as they may contain information relevant to the case such as files, photos and videos, call records, and geolocations.

The **Mobile Phone Examiner (MPE)** is a solution for mobile forensics that delivers an intuitive and simple interface, data visualization, and smart device support in a single forensic interface. MPE images integrate seamlessly with the FTK, allowing you to correlate evidence from multiple mobile devices with evidence from multiple computers within a single interface.

The following is a sample of smartphone analysis with MPE:

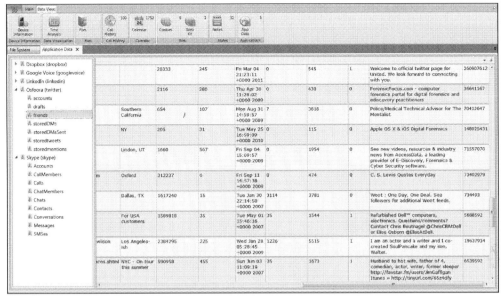

Summary

This chapter covered the main features of the new version of the Forensics Tool Kit. Activities that usually take a long time to execute can be performed in a much simpler way with the help of these new features.

The FTK 5 is a complete platform for the acquisition and analysis of many different types of digital media, and enables the extraction of evidence quickly and efficiently. Its new features provide an integrated and easy-to-use platform to help in the examiner's work.

The next chapter will discuss in detail the tool that cracks and recovers passwords, PRTK.

7
Working with PRTK

This chapter will cover the **Password Recovery Toolkit (PRTK)** and **Distributed Network Attack (DNA)**. Both are used to provide a password-cracking function. You can use PRTK and DNA in computer forensic investigations to access password-protected files or system passwords.

The main difference between these tools is that PRTK runs on a single machine only and DNA uses multiple machines across the network.

You will understand this difference and how to use the tools for the password recovery of a large number of popular software applications.

An overview of PRTK

The use of encryption and data protection through the use of passwords has steadily grown among the users of computers. Encryption is seen as a strategic business issue and is adopted by most companies.

Given this scenario, PRTK becomes a fundamental tool to assist in the digital investigation process, supporting the attempt to access the protected data contained in the evidence.

You can download the latest stable version of PRTK and DNA at `http://www.accessdata.com/support/product-downloads`.

PRTK supports a wide variety of products for password cracking. To access the full list of supported products and types of attack, click on **Help** and then click on **Recovery Modules**.

The following figure shows a small example of the supported products:

Module Name	Display Name	Attack Types	Supported Products
ABICoder	ABICoder Password Module	dictionary	Product Name: ABI Coder Versions supported: 3.5.7.4 - 3.6.1.4
Access	MS Access Password Module	decryption dictionary	Product Name: Microsoft Access Versions supported: Through 2013
ACT	ACT! Password Module	decryption	Product Name: ACT! Versions supported: 1 - 4 2000 5 - 6
AdvancedFileLock	AdvancedFileLock Password Module	dictionary	Product Name: Advanced File Lock Versions supported: 6 - 7.1
AIM	AIM Password Module	decryption dictionary	Product Name: AOL Instant Messenger Versions supported: Through 7.5 Product Name: AIM Triton Versions supported: Through 1.5 Product Name: AIM For Windows Versions supported: Through
AmiPro	AmiPro Password Module	dictionary	Product Name: Ami Pro Versions supported: *Unknown*

Understanding the PRTK interface

The PRTK interface is very simple and has a few options. The process is basically automatic and does not require much user intervention. The main functions of the interface are as follows:

- **Menu**: Through this, you can access all the functionalities and options for configuration and tuning.
- **Toolbar**: This provides quick access to the main features of the tool.
- **View All**: This is the main viewer. You can track the status of the password-cracking attack.

- **Properties**: This is where you can view information about a file in the attack process.

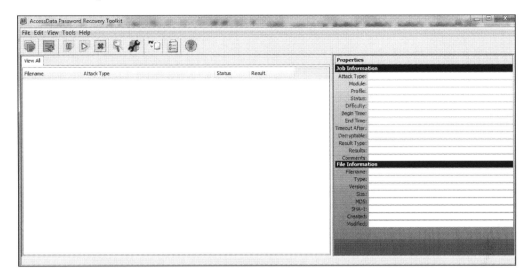

The main features and configurations will be discussed in the following topics.

Creating and managing dictionaries

Dictionaries are an optimization tool used for password recovery. By using dictionaries, specific candidate passwords are tested before the more general ones. This utility creates a variety of custom dictionaries for use with PRTK.

 Create backups of the word lists and dictionaries because if the dictionary is modified or deleted, you cannot recover it again.

The dictionary utility can be used to create or modify several types of dictionaries.

To use the dictionary utility, perform the following steps:

1. Click on **Tools** and then click on **Dictionary Tools**.

2. The **AccessData Dictionary Import Utility** screen will appear. Click on **Dictionary Tools** again.

3. Select the specific tool that you need to use (listed in the following table).

The following table lists tools that can be accessed from the **Dictionary Tools** menu and their functions:

Tool	Function
Dictionary Browser	To view the words in each dictionary or to delete a particular dictionary or dictionaries
Dictionary Info	To view specific details about a dictionary, such as the dictionary type, encoding, language, word count, and description
Biographical Dictionary Generator	Builds the dictionaries of candidate passwords from a collection of biographical details and from combinations of the biographical data entered
Pass-phrase Dictionary Generator	Builds dictionaries from a phrase file and using subphrases from the phrase file
Permutation Dictionary Generator	Builds dictionaries from a wordlist file and using the permutations of words from the wordlist file
Standard Dictionary Generator	Builds custom dictionaries using a wordlist file
Golden Dictionary Merge	Merges two golden dictionaries into a single golden dictionary

> The Biographical Dictionary is very useful for cracking passwords because it is very common for people to create their passwords based on the combinations of their personal information.

Starting a session for password recovery

The utilization of the password recovery tool is very simple. With a few clicks, your password cracking session is ready and running.

Managing profiles

To use PRTK for processing a password recovery, you need to select an appropriate profile for your case investigation. A profile is a set of specific rules that must be used to define which types of password recovery will be used.

You can use any of the default profiles or create your own.

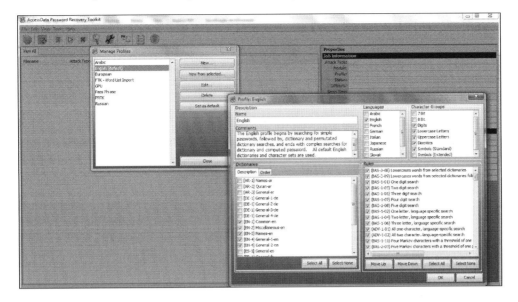

 By convention, this book uses the default profile **English**.

To start a new session of password cracking, perform the following steps:

1. Go to **File | Add Files** or click on the corresponding button on the toolbar as shown in the following screenshot.

2. Select the protected file and click on **Add**.

3. The suggested types of attacks will appear. You can change the type if necessary or leave the default model presented.

4. Click on **Finish** to start the cracking process.

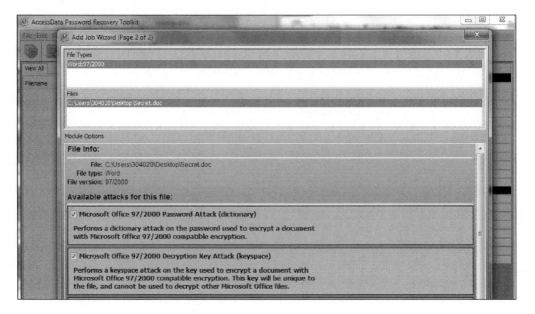

The cracking process will start, and you can follow the progress status of each of the techniques.

The time for obtaining the password can vary greatly depending on the complexity of the software application or the algorithm used for the password.

Additionally, the process for password cracking depends largely on the capability of the hardware, mainly the processor. There is specific equipment for the activity of cryptanalysis, which uses video cards (GPU) to gain speed.

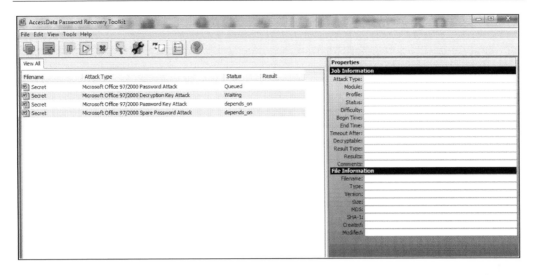

Note that the process is fully automated, requiring few interactions or modifications.

 You can use the drag-and-drop command to add files to PRTK.

DNA

As discussed earlier, the process of password cracking requires a lot of hardware resources.

DNA is a tool that can assist in this process since it uses sharing and distribution between the computers on the network resource.

DNA has an interface that is very similar to PRTK features with an exception of solution architecture.

There are two components to the DNA system as follows:

- **Supervisor**: This is a machine that controls the Worker machines in the DNA system and the jobs that they process. Install it before the Workers.

- **Worker**: This is responsible for processing jobs for decryption or password cracking. You should run the appropriate Worker installation program on each machine in the system.

Summary

This chapter covered the first steps to use the PRTK Forensics tool and a brief vision of the DNA solution.

Even though a simple solution of using their resources is extremely advanced, it can recover passwords from almost all commonly used files.

PRTK is a mandatory tool used in digital investigations since you will most likely find some protected files that may contain the key to the outcome of your investigation.

Index

SHA-1 Hash option 47
SHA-256 Hash option 47
single-node enterprise
   about 75
   using 75-77
Standard Dictionary Generator
   function 86
static analysis 79
Supervisor 89
Supplementary Files option 59
system files 54

T

threat analysis 79
Timeline Bookmark option 59
Time Zone
   changing 53, 54
   setting 33
Time Zone option 44
toolbar, FTK Imager interface 16

V

view panes, FTK Imager interface 17
volatile data 77

W

Windows registry files
   structure 28, 29
Worker 89 ,

[PACKT] Thank you for buying
PUBLISHING **Computer Forensics with FTK**

About Packt Publishing

Packt, pronounced 'packed', published its first book "*Mastering phpMyAdmin for Effective MySQL Management*" in April 2004 and subsequently continued to specialize in publishing highly focused books on specific technologies and solutions.

Our books and publications share the experiences of your fellow IT professionals in adapting and customizing today's systems, applications, and frameworks. Our solution based books give you the knowledge and power to customize the software and technologies you're using to get the job done. Packt books are more specific and less general than the IT books you have seen in the past. Our unique business model allows us to bring you more focused information, giving you more of what you need to know, and less of what you don't.

Packt is a modern, yet unique publishing company, which focuses on producing quality, cutting-edge books for communities of developers, administrators, and newbies alike. For more information, please visit our website: www.packtpub.com.

Writing for Packt

We welcome all inquiries from people who are interested in authoring. Book proposals should be sent to author@packtpub.com. If your book idea is still at an early stage and you would like to discuss it first before writing a formal book proposal, contact us; one of our commissioning editors will get in touch with you.

We're not just looking for published authors; if you have strong technical skills but no writing experience, our experienced editors can help you develop a writing career, or simply get some additional reward for your expertise.

Instant Wireshark Starter

ISBN: 978-1-84969-564-0   Paperback: 68 pages

A quick and easy guide to getting started with network analysis using Wireshark

1. Learn something new in an Instant! A short, fast, focused guide delivering immediate results.

2. Documents key features and tasks that can be performed using Wireshark.

3. Covers details of filters, statistical analysis, and other important tasks.

4. Also includes advanced topics like decoding captured data, name resolution, and reassembling.

Instant Kali Linux

ISBN: 978-1-84969-566-4   Paperback: 68 pages

A quick guide to learn the most widely-used operation system by network security professionals

1. Learn something new in an Instant! A short, fast, focused guide delivering immediate results.

2. Covers over 30 different tools included in Kali Linux.

3. Easy guide to set up and install Kali Linux under different hardware sets.

4. Step-by-step examples to get started with pen-testing tools.

Please check **www.PacktPub.com** for information on our titles

Printed in Great Britain
by Amazon.co.uk, Ltd.,
Marston Gate.